WALES

IN COLOUR

WALES

IN COLOUR

REBECCA KING

DIAL
HOUSE

CONTENTS

GWENT   7

GLAMORGAN   16

DYFED   24

POWYS   36

GWYNEDD   49

CLWYD   72

First published 1995

ISBN 0 7110 2372 7

© Ian Allan Ltd 1995

Published by Dial House

an imprint of Ian Allan Ltd, Terminal House, Station Approach, Shepperton, Surrey TW17 8AS.
Printed by Ian Allan Printing Ltd, Coombelands House, Coombelands Lane, Addlestone, Weybridge, Surrey KT15 1HY.

Front cover:
Carew Castle, Dyfed
Originally a medieval stronghold, Carew Castle was turned into a mansion in Tudor times. The ruins stand beside a tidal creek of the Carew River, and to the west of the castle is a restored working tidal mill dating back to the 16th century.

Back cover:
Llanberis Pass, Gwynedd
Regarded as one of the bleakest valleys in Wales, the Llanberis Pass cuts through the rock on the northeast flank of the Snowdon range. Llanberis village is where many people begin their ascent of Snowdon either on foot (this is the easiest of the six traditional routes to the summit), or by the Snowdon Mountain Railway which runs more or less alongside the footpath.

Frontispiece:
The Brecon Beacons, Powys
Seen here beyond Llyn-cwm-llwch are two of the most popular peaks in the Brecon Beacons National Park — Pen-y-Fan and Corn Du. They stand about half a mile from each other and are the highest peaks in the Park, with the aptly named Pen-y-Fan (it means 'Top of the Park') pipping Corn Du by a few feet. A well-worn route to the peaks starts just south of Storey Arms on the A470.

Left:
Pistyll Rhaeadr, Clwyd
A view of the falls.

Opposite:
Laugharne, Dyfed
The Boathouse.

All photographs by the AA Photo Library.

INTRODUCTION

Whereas on the one hand Wales is an integral part of the United Kingdom with no formal border, on the other it is a country with its own culture, language, traditions and history which become apparent as soon as the Marches are left behind.

Among this country's most obvious charms — and one which draws a high percentage of the annual visitors — is undoubtedly the unspoilt beauty and diversity of its landscape. This takes the form of spectacular mountain ranges, sparkling lakes and reservoirs, lush river valleys, sweeping sandy beaches and stretches of more rugged coastline.

Wales is not a large country — it measures some 160 miles from north to south and 50 miles across from the coast to the English border, a total of 8,000 square miles — but with a population of only 2.8 million and about 60 per cent of that concentrated in the heavily industrialised southeast, the majority of it is relatively sparsely populated.

Much of the country's most beautiful countryside falls within the three national parks. In the southwest is the Pembrokeshire Coast National Park, which, as its name suggests, hugs the coastline from St Dogmaels to Amroth and provides glorious walking with wild flowers and sea birds in abundance; eastwards is the land-locked Brecon Beacons National Park, drawing serious hill walkers from far and wide but in particular from the Midlands and southeast Wales; and to the northwest is the Snowdonia National Park, possibly the most famous of Britain's (let alone Wales') national parks, boasting as it does the highest mountain in Wales and England, plus spectacular walking and climbing routes safeguarded for the most part by the National Trust and the Forestry Commission. Then there is the underground world of caves and caverns, potholes and fissures in south Wales.

Set against this backdrop of natural grandeur are the legacies of Wales' past. First and foremost among these must be the numerous great castles that rank among Europe's finest, ranging from the huge concentric fortresses built by Edward I in the 13th and 14th centuries around the north coast and in whose shadow market towns grew up, to 19th-century splendours such as Cardiff Castle. Edward's castles succeeded the motte-and-bailey structures introduced by the Normans in the 12th century, remains of which can still be seen. The Normans were also responsible for establishing religious buildings such as Tintern Abbey and Strata Florida, and the evocative ruins of those too still grace the countryside. Older yet are the prehistoric remains that litter the Preseli Hills and Anglesey in particular, and what the Romans left behind.

Wales' industrial heritage — slate quarrying and mining; silver, lead, copper and gold mining — is also much in evidence, with a great deal of what is left having been turned into imaginative tourist attractions, both above and below ground. With the Industrial Revolution came a need to transport raw materials to the coast and the narrow-gauge steam railways, designed to haul stone and slate down the steep narrow valleys, are now one of the most famous features of Wales — The Great Little Trains of Wales.

Towns and villages are no less diverse: Victorian spa towns, remote mountain villages, bustling seaside resorts catering for the

holiday-maker, medieval towns encircled with great walls — they are all here to be explored along with attendant museums, churches and important houses.

Last but not least is the culture and language of Wales, epitomised by the Royal National Eisteddfod — an annual celebration of poetry, drama and music — but also an intrinsic part of everyday life. Many road signs and place names are in both Welsh and English, and Welsh is widely spoken, particularly in mid and north Wales.

When all these ingredients are combined the cliché 'Wales has something to offer everyone' springs to mind; cliché it may be, but it is also true.

Many of the places of interest in Wales, ranging from abbeys to protected areas of the countryside, are either in the care of CADW: Welsh Historic Monuments, or the National Trust. Membership of both can be obtained. The Wales Tourist Board has a wealth of information and printed material about what to do and see in Wales.

Wales Tourist Board
Brunel House, 2 Fitzalan Road, Cardiff CF2 1UY
Tel: 01222 499909

CADW
Brunel House, 2 Fitzalan Road, Cardiff CF2 1UY
Tel: 01222 465511

National Trust
Trinity Square, Llandudno LL30 2DE
Tel: 01492 860123

Above:
St David's, Dyfed
The cathedral of St David's and the ruins of the Bishop's Palace, which lie near by on the other side of the River Alun, reign supreme at the heart of this tiny 'city'. A church was first founded here by St David, the patron saint of Wales, in about the middle of the 1st century, but the oldest parts of the present building are probably no earlier than the 2nd century. St David is reputed to have been born half a mile south at St Non's Bay, where there is a tiny ruined chapel commemorating the fact. On 1 March a service is held in the cathedral to honour St David.

Above:
Caerwent
Known to the Romans as *Venta Silurum*, meaning 'the market town of the Silures', Caerwent is unusual in that it was just that, and not a military base as was more often the case with Roman settlements. Remnants of the walls — of which the south wall is the most complete — surround the village. Many of the items discovered during excavations can be seen in the museums at Newport and Caerleon.

Opposite:
Wye Gorge
The Wye Valley Walk, a 52-mile long-distance footpath, follows the River Wye between Hereford and Chepstow along clearly marked and well-maintained paths. The section of the route seen here passes near the base of famous Symonds Yat Rock — a spectacular 500ft-high viewpoint in a loop of the river.

Above:
Chepstow Castle
Chepstow Castle has stood guard over one of the most important routes into Wales since the Normans built it some 10 years after the Conquest; it was their first stone castle in Wales. Protected to the north and east by a loop of the Wye, the 13th-century Port Wall (still in evidence) enclosed the medieval port that developed to the south and west.

9

Above:
Sugar Loaf Mountain
Footpaths criss-cross the 2,000-plus acres of Sugar Loaf Mountain that belong to the National Trust and routes lead up to the highest point (1,955ft), from where there are wonderful views across the Bristol Channel to the south and the Malvern Hills to the northeast. The mountain — actually an extinct volcano — lies to the northwest of Abergavenny in the foothills of the Black Mountains.

Opposite:
Tintern Abbey
Founded on the banks of the Wye by Cistercian monks in 1131, the abbey was rebuilt between the 13th and 15th centuries when it reached the height of its prosperity; the ruins seen today date mainly from that period. From the 18th century, Tintern began to attract lovers of the 'picturesque', including Wordsworth and Turner, and it became a highlight of the Wye Tour — a fashionable boat trip between Ross-on-Wye and Chepstow that attracted a cult following.

Opposite:
River Wye
There are excellent views of the meandering Wye from the look-out point known as Eagle's Nest, 700ft above the river near the Wynd Cliff, north of Chepstow. During the early 19th century, 365 steps were built into the cliff here as a tourist attraction.

Above:
Raglan Castle
Distinguished as the last medieval fort to be built in Britain, Raglan Castle is an impressive ruin. The Great Tower, dating from the 15th century, occupies the original motte built after Gwent was conquered by the Normans in the 11th century. Although partially destroyed by Fairfax during the Civil War, the tower can still be climbed and it is worth doing so for the fine views.

13

Right:
White Castle
With Skenfrith and Grosmont, White
Castle formed what is known as the
Welsh Trilateral — a defensive
triangle of castles built by the
Normans to protect the borderlands
and the route into south Wales.
White Castle gained its name from
the white plaster rendering which
covered it.

Opposite:
Tredegar House
This handsome red-brick mansion,
two miles east of Newport, dates
from the mid-17th century when it
was rebuilt to replace an earlier
home of the Morgan family. During
the Regency period the house became
a fashionable haunt of high society —
including royalty. Now in the hands
of the local council, the interior of
Tredegar has been well restored and
the grounds feature a bird garden, a
boating and fishing lake, craft
workshops and an orangery.

Opposite:
Nash Point
The limestone platforms below the dramatic shale and limestone layered cliffs of Nash Point, west of Llanwit Major, are only revealed at low tide. This beautiful stretch of coastline is part of the Heritage Coast, and an information centre with details of walks and drives can be found at Dunrevan beach.

Left:
Dyffryn Gardens
Over 55 acres here are devoted to an arboretum, a wild area, formal gardens, a palmhouse, conservatories, small 'theme' gardens, a butterfly house and sweeping lawns. Having bought the estate in 1891, a coal magnate built the house and proceeded to develop the grounds into what they are today.

Following page:
Cardiff Castle
At the heart of Wales' capital city is its castle, buildings that have grown and evolved from the time the Romans first built a fort here. Now a striking centrepiece to the city with its 150ft-high clock tower, visitors flock to see the exuberant work of eccentric architect and designer William Burges who was employed by the immensely wealthy 3rd Marquess of Bute to restore the castle. Other attractions are the two regimental museums, the battlements with their views of the city and the 11th-century keep.

17

Left:
Caerphilly Castle
Covering a site of over 30 acres, and surrounded by an enormous moat, Caerphilly is the largest castle in Wales. It was also the first concentric castle to be built in Britain, ie with an inner system of defences overlooking an outer system, a design which Edward I subsequently made his own. Caerphilly has not always looked so splendid, however. Cromwell drained the moat during the Civil War and by the beginning of this century a mish-mash of buildings occupied the moat and castle precincts. Fortunately, in 1958 these were demolished and the moat reflooded.

Above:
Rhossili
The sands facing Rhossili Bay at the western end of the Gower Peninsula sweep round in a five-mile curve. Behind, Rhossili Down stretches for about two miles, reaching its highest point at The Beacon (633ft) to the south. About 500 acres here are owned by the National Trust.

Opposite:
Swansea
After suffering severe bomb damage during World War 2, Swansea rose phoenix-like from the ashes and today it is a thriving modern city trying to shake off its industrial image. It reached its heyday as an industrial port in the 18th century when it became Wales' largest port. Now the old docks are a centrepiece of a new marina.

Right:
Vale of Neath
The Aberdulais Falls on the Dulais River have been a popular beauty spot since the 18th century and a number of landscape artists, including Turner, have painted them. It is estimated that about 35 million gallons of water crash over the rocks here, and this power was first harnessed in the late 16th century. Starting with copper smelting, the Falls have since powered a corn mill, ironworks and tin-plate works.

Opposite:
Three Cliffs Bay
About a mile from Parkmill, on the southern side of the Gower, the Penard Pil valley winds down to the sea at Three Cliffs Bay. The Gower was the first area to be designated an Area of Outstanding Natural Beauty (AONB) and is renowned for its wild flowers and sea birds. The National Trust owns about 5,000 acres of the peninsula in all.

Above:

Talley Abbey

Founded in the 12th century for Premonstratensian monks, Talley Abbey was the only abbey in Wales of this Order. It suffered badly at the hands of Owain Glyndwr and by the Dissolution it had all but been abandoned. The skeletal ruins stand near two small lakes in the Dulais Valley: Talley comes from Tal-y-Llychan, meaning 'head of the lakes.'

Opposite:

Pembroke Castle

Standing on the south bank of the Pembroke River, which flows into the huge natural harbour of Milford Haven, is the old county town of Pembroke and former capital of 'Little England Beyond Wales.' The enormous castle, surrounded on three sides by water, is dominated by a 75ft-high circular keep which has walls 19ft thick at the base. Beneath the castle is a huge natural cavern called the Wogan, which was probably used as a store room. It can either be reached down a flight of stairs from inside the castle, or via a path skirting the outside walls.

Opposite:
Cors Caron Nature Reserve
North of Tregaron the River Teifi
flows through the Cors Caron
Nature Reserve. Covering about
three square miles, the reserve
includes three peat bogs which
are lightly domed in shape, giving
them the name 'raised' peat bogs.
These bogs have taken thousands
of years to form and, despite
destruction as a result of peat
cutting (banned in the 1960s), have
remained intact in places.

Left:
Tenby
The lively and attractive old resort
of Tenby is familiar as a resting
place to many who have walked the
Pembrokeshire Coast Path. Below
Castle Hill, (where there is a statue
of Prince Albert, the castle ruins and
the town museum and art gallery,)
the town is a picturesque jumble of
alleyways, whitewashed stone
houses, steps and cobbles.
   On either side of the headland is a
sandy beach and there are boat trips
to Caldey Island, home of a Trappist
monastery, from the harbour.

27

Above:

Llanstephan Castle

Built between the 11th and 13th centuries, the ruins of Llanstephan Castle stand impressively on the west bank of the Twyi estuary. From the towers there are views in all directions and its strategic importance is obvious.

Opposite:

Laugharne

Dylan Thomas has made Laugharne, an otherwise unremarkable little town on the Taf estuary, famous. The poet lived here for the four years prior to his untimely death (brought about by alcohol abuse), drawing inspiration from the peace and beauty he found at his home here by the water's edge. Now known as the Dylan Thomas Boathouse, the house — and the old garage in which he used to write — is a museum, art gallery and tea room.

Little now survives of the castle around which the town grew, but the ruins are picturesque enough.

Opposite:
Black Mountain
Not to be confused with the Black Mountains at the eastern side of the Brecon Beacons National Park, the Black Mountain is at the western extremity of the Park. Even more confusingly, it is not, as its name suggests, a single mountain but an upland range stretching northwards from Brynamman. Many claim this unpopulated area provides the most exhilarating walking in South Wales.

Above:
Kidwelly Castle
Roger, Bishop of Salisbury, built a priory and castle at Kidwelly at the beginning of the 12th century. Both the priory, a dependency of Sherborne Abbey in Dorset, and the original castle have disappeared and the oldest part of the castle surviving today is the 13th-century rectangular inner ward. Never extensively restored, Kidwelly's medieval remains are remarkably intact.

31

Opposite and left:
Manorbier
Overlooking the bay of the same name (opposite), the village of Manorbier has gained fame as the birthplace of clergyman, writer and traveller Giraldus Cambrensis (Gerald of Wales) whose books, *The Journey Through Wales* and *The Description of Wales*, are vivid and perceptive records of 12th-century Wales.

From the churchyard (left) there is a good view of the castle, a 14th-century fortified manor house. An effigy of Walter de Barri, half-brother of Giraldus, can be seen in the church.

33

Right:
Dinas Nature Reserve
Since 1968 the RSPB has owned about 100 acres around Dinas, a cone-shaped hill at the junction of the Tywi and Doethie rivers. An information centre, plus footpaths and a wooden boardwalk across the bog in the Tywi Gorge, make this an interesting and accessible reserve. Glimpses of the famous red kite (confined in Britain to Wales) flying over in spring or winter are not unusual.

Opposite:
Pentre Ifan
There is no shortage of prehistoric remains in the Preseli Hills, but Pentre Ifan, reached from a side road three miles east of Nevern, is one of the most impressive with its 16ft capstone. Dating from about 2000bc, this megalithic tomb would originally been covered with a mound of earth.

Right and opposite:
Elan Valley
In the 1890s a series of reservoirs was built in the Elan Valley to supply water to Birmingham and the West Midlands. Previously an unknown area of rocky hillsides and woodland, it has become known as the Lakeland of Wales and is nearly as much visited as its English counterpart. There are four man-made lakes in all in the Elan Valley, each with an impressive dam, and all can be viewed from roads alongside their shores. The Caban Coch reservoir (opposite) submerged the home of Shelley and his wife along with several other houses and buildings when the valley was flooded.

To the west is the newest reservoir, the Claerwen, which fills a separate valley (right). This is a less popular area than the Elan Valley and provides good, serious walking.

Right:
Elan Valley
The Penygarreg reservoir dam holds back the water of the river Elan.

Opposite:
Usk Reservoir
Completed in the mid-1950s, Usk is the most recent of the reservoirs that have been built within the boundaries of the Brecon Beacons National Park and are now an integral part of the landscape. A footpath encircles the peaceful lake, and anglers can fish for trout — with a permit.

Glasfynydd Forest stretches away from the shore and here walkers are well provided for too, with a number of marked trails to choose from.

Above and opposite :
Tretower
The Usk Valley village of Tretower has two places of interest: one is Tretower Court (above), an attractive late medieval manor house, and the other is

Tretower Castle (opposite), built by the Normans to defend the Rhiangoll glen. The Court has family rooms and a Great Hall ranged round a central cobbled courtyard. Despite many alterations over the years a number of the original details have survived.

Above:
Y Gaer
Y Gaer, meaning 'The Fort', was built by the Romans in the 1st century AD at the hub of a network of roads radiating out to other forts. As such it was a large and important site, not finally abandoned until late into the 3rd century. Later, much of the stone went into the building of Brecon Castle, three miles east.

Opposite:
Powis Castle
This National Trust property just south of Welshpool is one of Wales' greatest treasures. A castle in name only, it was transformed into an Elizabethan mansion in the late 16th century. Welsh architect William Winde designed the beautiful gardens, which descend in huge terraces from the house. As well as outstanding plasterwork, furniture and paintings, there is the Clive Museum, a collection of Indian and Far Eastern memorabilia assembled by 'Clive of India' (whose son married into the family who owned Powis Castle).

Right:

Ystradfellte

Towards the southern boundary of the Brecon Beacons National Park there is an area of limestone and millstone grit where erosion of the soluble limestone by the rivers Melte, Hepste and Neath has produced spectacular waterfalls and a fascinating underground world of caves and potholes.

West of Ystradfellte are the Dan-yr-Ogof Showcaves — possibly the largest cave system in western Europe. Despite being very touristy, these spectacular and well-lit caverns with their lakes, stalactites and stalagmites are well worth a visit.

Opposite:

Maen Madoc

Rising from the lonely, windswept moorland of Fforest Fawr is the 9ft-high standing stone, Maen Madoc. Although thought to be prehistoric, it has a later Latin inscription. The stone stands on the Sarn Helen Roman road which linked south Wales with the north coast. Sarn Helen means Helen's Causeway, and there has naturally been much speculation as to who Helen was. Directly north of Maen Madoc is another such stone, Maen Lila; this is 12ft high and 9ft across.

Opposite and above:
Views from Gospel Pass and Hay Bluff
Hay Bluff (2,219ft), just by Offa's Dyke and the Welsh border, south of Hay-on-Wye, is a magnificent viewpoint northwards over the Wye Valley and across to Mynydd Eppynt to the south.

Going south towards the Black Mountains the road rises to Gospel Pass before dropping down into the Vale of Ewyas. The English name is thought to have evolved during the 12th century when Giraldus Cambrensis travelled Wales preaching and raising money for the Third Crusade.

47

Above:

Llangorse Lake

The second largest natural lake in Wales after Bala, and relatively shallow; reed-fringed Llangorse Lake has become a great watersports centre with rowing, canoeing, windsurfing and yachting on offer. Prehistoric lake dwellings have been found near the shore here, and a dug-out canoe dating from the 1st century was rescued in 1925; it can now be seen in the Brecknock Museum at Brecon. A number of myths regarding the lake have evolved over the centuries, with tales of tolling bells and drowned cities, witches and blood-coloured water.

Left:
Conwy Castle
Thomas Telford's elegant suspension bridge, built over the River Conwy in the early 19th century to replace a ferry crossing, was designed to complement Edward I's splendid 21-towered castle.

Following page:
Gwernan Lake and Cadair Idris
The massif of Cadair Idris can be seen here rising up behind Gwernan Lake, south of Dollgellau. Clear lakes, precipitous drops and stunning views await anyone wanting to explore this demanding walking country. A number of routes of varying length and difficulty can be taken up on to the peaks of Cadair Idris, which fall just short of 3,000ft.

GWYNEDD

Above:
Holy Island
At the westernmost tip of Holy Island, off the west coast of Anglesey, are the South Stack cliffs. Here seabirds wheel and scream in huge colonies — the RSPB has a reserve here — and climbers tackle the sheer rock-faces. Below, the lighthouse of 1808, which was designed by the architect of Dartmoor Prison, can be reached by a narrow bridge.

Opposite:

Caernarfon Castle

Edward I commissioned James of St George to build the magnificent castle at Caernarfon on the banks of the Seiont in 1283. Distinguished by its polygonal towers and layers of coloured stone, the castle is actually little more than a shell now. It forms one side of the town walls which are nearly half a mile in length and shelter houses dating from the 16th to the 19th centuries.

HRH Prince Charles was invested here in 1969 as Prince of Wales, a title bestowed on the eldest son of the monarch since the days of Edward I.

Left:

Portmeirion

Pastel-coloured buildings, flower-filled streets and a riot of architectural styles and detail are the ingredients Welsh architect Sir Clough Williams-Ellis used to create this fairytale village that looks as if it should be in the Mediterranean rather than on the north coast of Wales. As well as the attraction of the buildings themselves, there is also a pottery, craft shops, a museum and miles of footpaths flanked by rhododendrons. Privately-owned, the village is open to day visitors and has a number of self-catering cottages as well as an hotel.

53

Right and opposite:
The Lleyn
The Lleyn, meaning 'peninsula', (opposite) stretches for about 25 miles towards the Irish Sea between Caernarfon Bay and Cardigan Bay. It is an Area of Outstanding Natural Beauty. Sandy beaches and seaside resorts along the south coast of the peninsula attract summer visitors and there are several prehistoric remains inland.

Two miles off the tip of The Lleyn is Bardsey Island (right), Ynys Enlli in Welsh, which means the Isle of Currents. Historically a place of pilgrimage since the 6th century, most visitors today make the choppy boat trip across Bardsea Sound to the island, now a nature reserve, to bird-watch.

Opposite:
Bodnant Garden
A profusion of rhododendrons, camellias and magnolias in spring; roses, hydrangeas and herbaceous borders in summer and lovely colours from the shrubs and trees in autumn plus the bonus of lovely views of Snowdonia, make this National Trust property a year-round delight. The 'pin mill' at the end of the lily pool, originally built as a summerhouse and later used as a pin factory, was brought to Bodnant in 1939 and restored as a garden feature.

Above:
Criccieth
A popular family resort that developed in Victorian days on the south coast of The Lleyn, Criccieth sprawls below its ruined 13th-century castle perched up on a ridge between two large bays. Views from here encompass Harlech across the water and Snowdonia to the northeast.

David Lloyd George (prime minister from 1916 until 1922) lived at nearby Llanystumdy as a boy.

57

Right and Opposite:
Newborough Warren
The 600-acre sand dunes of Newborough Warren (right) on Anglesey sweep round to Llanddwyn Island (it is, in fact, only cut off at high tide) where the remains of the church dedicated to St Dwynwen, Welsh patron saint of lovers, can be found (opposite). Corsican and Monterey pine now cover much of the land behind the dunes which has been designated a National Nature Reserve.

Malltraeth Sands, north of Llanddwyn, was a favourite haunt of C. F. Tunnicliffe, famous for his exquisite paintings of birds.

Opposite:
Beddgelert
Set at the heart of the Snowdonia National Park and at the junction of three river valleys, Beddgelert is an ideal base for exploring the mountains; a number of good walks start from here.

Above:
Precipice Walk
This misleadingly named walk, encircling Foel Cynwch, northwest of Dolgellau, draws many people because of the outstanding views which can be enjoyed virtually all the way around the far from precipitous three-mile circuit. They include Cadair Idris and the Mawddach estuary.

Above:
Tryfan
Some claim conical-shaped Tryfan in the Ogwen Valley is the most challenging of Snowdonia's mountains. It is renowned for its twin peaks — Adam and Eve — at the summit; climbers traditionally jump from one to the other, a distance of some five feet. The National Trust owns Tryfan, along with nine of the other main peaks over 3,000ft in North Wales.

Opposite:
Llyn Crafnant
Llyn Crafnant is one of the two reservoirs that can be reached from Trefriw along a narrow lane. The lake, 603ft deep, serves Trefriw, a town associated with Llewelyn the Great who lived here. Today, the woollen mill, with its large shop, is a popular attraction.

Right and opposite:
Beaumaris
Dating from the end of the 13th century, Beaumaris Castle (opposite) was the last fortress to be built by Edward I. Concentric in design and surrounded by a once-tidal moat, the extensive ruins stand by the shore at the edge of the town which takes its name from the area dubbed 'beautiful marsh'.

From the pier (right) there are views across the Menai Strait, first bridged by Telford's great suspension bridge in the 1820s. In summer yachtsmen gather here for the annual regatta.

Above:
Dinas Mawddwy
Popular as a centre for walkers and anglers, Dinas Mawddwy sits at the junction of the Dyfi and Cerist rivers in southern Snowdonia surrounded by wooded hills. Rhododendrons are a glorious feature of the nearby slopes in springtime.

Opposite:
Roman Steps
It is not known for certain when or why this stairway of flat, uneven slabs known as Roman Steps was built, but it is more likely to be medieval than Roman and probably formed part of a track used by drovers or traders. The steps lie in the valley of the Artro, about four miles east of Llanbedr beyond Llyn Cwm Bychan, a remote lake on the edge of the Rhinogs. This rocky moorland, rising to about 2,500ft, is a true wilderness.

Opposite and Left:
Snowdonia
There are nearly 2,000 miles of
designated paths in the Snowdonia
National Park, including many of
Wales' most challenging mountain
routes. Carred Moel-Siabod
(opposite) rises to the north of
Dolwyddelan and Y Garn (left) to
the east of Llanberis.

69

Opposite:
Cwm Idwal
Sculpted by glaciers, Cwm Idwal is of great interest from a geological and wildlife point of view. It was designated a nature reserve — the first in Wales — in 1954. Carnedd Dafydd, rising up behind the lake, and Carnedd Llewelyn near by, are the two highest mountains in Wales after Snowdon.

Left:
Harlech
Dramatically sited on a 200ft-high bluff, Harlech Castle is well named: Harlech means 'bold rock'. Another of Edward's concentric fortifications, it was begun in 1283 and completed six years later. The main feature here is the three-storey-high gatehouse where an exhibition is now housed.

72

Above:
Rhuddlan Castle
Formerly a Welsh royal seat, Rhuddlan Castle is historically important as the place where Edward I signed the statute of Rhuddlan in 1284 which subjugated Wales to England. The great drum towers — the work of James of St George — are still impressive.

Below:
Pistyll Rhaeadr
Claimed to be Wales' highest waterfall and dubbed one of the 'Seven Wonders of Wales', Pistyll Rhaeadr, on the border of Clwyd and Powys, is made up of waters from the Berwyn Mountains. The Falls plunge over a sheer cliff and flow through a natural arch known as the Fairy Bridge into a deep basin. They have been a tourist attraction since they were discovered by George Borrow, traveller, linguist and author of *Wild Wales,* in the mid-19th century.

73

Opposite:

Bodryhddan Hall

A house has stood on this site for over 700 years but the Bodryhddan Hall we see today is a far cry from the original humble dwelling. What has survived, however, are parts of the 15th-century house and these have been incorporated into the existing building which has grown over the centuries. Throughout these changes the Rowley-Conwys have owned the estate, as they do today. The Hall has a good collection of armour, paintings and furniture, and an ornamental garden.

Left:

Trevor Rocks

The dramatic limestone escarpment called Trevor Rocks lies to the northeast of Llangollen. Alongside are the Eglwyseg Rocks and from these heights there are superb views into the Vale of Llangollen and across the Berwyn Range to the south.

75

Opposite and Left:

Llangollen

Rail, road, river and canal run along the Dee Valley through Llangollen. The Llangollen Canal (opposite), a feeder to the Shropshire Union, draws its water from the Horseshoe Falls west of the town and these days is busy with barges carrying holiday-makers and day-trippers. The Llangollen Railway, seen here just outside Berwyn Halt, runs west from Llangollen along part of the old track-bed of the Barmouth-Ruabon line. There are plans to continue to Corwen. With full-size locomotives, the line recreates the days of the Great Western Railway.

Right:
Castell Dinas
Perched up above Llangollen at nearly 1,500ft, Castell Dinas was once the region's largest fortress; its name means 'Crow's Fortress Castle.' From the medieval ruins there are fine views along the valley in both directions which reward the stiff climb up. Partly surrounding the ruins are the earthworks of an Iron Age hillfort.

Opposite:
Flint Castle
This was the first fortress in Edward I's 'Iron Ring' — the chain of great castles, each a good day's march from the next, built around the north coast of Wales. Flint guarded the marshes of the Dee estuary and the important shipping lanes into Chester.

Left:
Tower
This fortified manor house just south of Mold has been in the same family for 500 years. Many alterations have been made to the house since it was built in the 15th century and today it is a charming blend of medieval features, 18th-century elegance and modern country-house comforts.